BOSSY PAR

Every year well over 1000 people ent[...]
Poetry Competition, which is staged b[...]
evening newspaper and now attracts £1500 in extra sponsorship
for poetry.

The top award in the junior section is the Athena Children's
Prize for Poetry. The winner's school receives £200 worth of
books from Athena in Gateshead, and the winning poem is
published in *Puffin News*.

The best poet in the 16 to 18 age group wins a week-long
writing course – sponsored by Bloodaxe Books – at the Arvon
Foundation's Lumb Bank writing centre in West Yorkshire. The
top 20 junior poets also win £15 individual book prizes given by
Athena, and a writing workshop with a Bloodaxe poet.

The competition is also sponsored by the Literary and
Philosophical Society in Newcastle, who provide the top prizes
in the adult section: the Basil Bunting Award of £400 for the best
poem and the Edward Boyle Poetry Prize of £250 for the most
promising new poet. Three runners-up win week-long Arvon
courses sponsored by Bloodaxe Books.

The Chronicle competition is the only one of its kind in the
country. The 20 winners in both the adult and the junior sections
all have their poems published in the paper, which has a
readership estimated at half a million.

The competition is judged each year by Chronicle editor
Graeme Stanton and Neil Astley of Bloodaxe with a leading
British poet or poets. This book features all the winning
children's poems by winners from the 1987 competition,
together with the best poems by winners from the previous
three years. The third competition judge in 1987 was Douglas
Dunn, and the poets judging the children's entries in the prev-
ious three years were Bob Pegg, Dick Davis and Ken Smith.

The book has been edited by Neil Astley, with the poets
contributing comments on themselves and their poems. The age
given above each title is the poet's age when the poem was
written.

BOSSY PARROT

THE BEST CHILDREN'S POEMS FROM THE
**EVENING CHRONICLE
POETRY COMPETITION**

BLOODAXE BOOKS

ISBN: 1 85224 040 7

First published 1987 by
Bloodaxe Books Ltd,
P.O. Box 1SN,
Newcastle upon Tyne NE99 1SN.

Bloodaxe Books Ltd acknowledges
the financial assistance of Northern Arts.

Typeset and printed in Great Britain by
Tyneside Free Press Workshop Ltd, Newcastle upon Tyne.

HELEN PERCY

Aged 10
If the World Was Crazy

If the world was crazy, you know what I'd eat?
A pushchair sandwich, a drink of meat,
A fork full of soup, and then I might try
A golliwog stew, or candy floss pie,
A felt-tip sausage, a worm jelly
That would wriggle and squiggle inside my belly.
A bowl full of mist from a day that was hazy,
That's what I'd eat if the world was crazy.

If the world was crazy, you know what I'd wear?
A dress made of dewdrops for when it was fair,
A paper hat and a paper coat,
And I'd sail away in a material boat.
With a dark, dark, red tie
Made from blackcurrant pie,
On my belt the buckle's a daisy,
That's what I'd wear if the world was crazy.

If the world was crazy, you know what I'd do?
I'd ride a sunbeam and live in stew,
I'd have backward knees and backward feet,
And then I'd buy a paper seat.
I'd say boo-hoo when I was glad,
And shout hurray! when I was sad.
And all the men would be so lazy
We'd abolish them if the world was crazy.

Helen Percy won first prize in the Chronicle competition in 1985 with this poem, which she wrote for English homework. She is now 12, lives in Dudley, near Cramlington, and goes to Dudley Middle School.

'I don't write poetry unless it's for school. We were given the title and we had to write 3 verses. I like rhyming poetry and am not so keen on the deep meaningful ones. I also like amusing poetry and I hate soppy love poems.'

IAIN MOFFAT

Iain Moffat was born in Scotland, and moved to Cramlington 4 years ago. Now 13, he has moved up from Stonelaw Middle School to Cramlington High.

'At school we were given the task of writing a poem called Heroes. *I came up with the first few lines and then continued. Another time we were told to write poems connected with school, and I thought of doing an acrostic. In a short while, after brief thinking, I came up with* Mathematics.*'*

Aged 11
Heroes

That old Antarctic Captain, he's "Scott" a lot
    of bottle,
His Cules did twelve brave tasks, or was it
    Her Cules?
The man called Mr Yuss could kill a Gorgon,
    I think he was Percy Yuss,
Old Titus needed porridge Oates to fight off
    his disease.

Back in olden Sherwood, a man was Robbin'
    Who'd call themselves rich
And elsewhere there's a Mother who tries
    "To raise a" dying man.
Someone who's really Super, man, is from
    the planet Krypton
As Geldof tries to raise a Bob for every
    dying African.

The man called Captain James, he could cook
    up a success,
And Hillary's muscles were Tensing as he climbed
    up Everest.
Who was a match for Swan, as North went
    very South?
There is no doubt about it, these heroes are
    the best.

Mathematics

Multiplication is like *deja vu* with figures, where the repetition ends.
Algebra is full of 'to the power of' and is an alloy of English and Maths.
Tables are the data in your mental computer, which sometimes slow it
  down.
Histograms: as simple as babies; with many blocks, often of many
  colours.
Equals signals similarities between an equation and an answer.
Measurements explain the dimensions of solids, liquids or gases, as
  discovered by you.
Addition makes an original bigger; it is like giving a house an extension.
Totals are achieved when two things merge together and expand.
Isosceles triangles have a pair of identical edges, as a pod has two
  identical peas.
Charts relay information in graphic form, though they are not always
  pictorial.
Subtraction lowers things by grabbing them, then taking some away.

ARANDA LOUISE BATESON

Aged 10
Loneliness

Loneliness is miserable
A frightening effect.
Cold, dark and gloomy
Locked in a dungeon forever
Dampened moss around the place,
Loneliness is me alone in my cell.

Loneliness is cold and dark
Cold stone to sit on
Cold stone for a bed
No heat at all
Never see the light of day
Loneliness is me alone in my cell.

Loneliness is me alone
For loneliness spreads fast
Cobwebs, mice and dark grey rats
My ragged clothes,
My poor old bones,
Loneliness is me alone in my cell.

Aranda Louise Bateson lives in Dudley, near Cramlington, and goes to Dudley Middle School. Now 12, she likes reading all poetry.

She wrote *Loneliness* after a school visit to Warkworth Castle: *'When we went to the cellars, I made a list of words about how I felt being in there, and wrote the poem around them.'*

STEVEN GRAHAM

Aged 14
Winter

Winter begins when
we see a mysterious
white weed which glistens
like sparkling jewels
that glow with unearthly light.
And it is this which
frightens my soul
with coldness.

Steven Graham is now 17, lives in Longbenton, and goes to Pendower Hall Special School in Newcastle.

'I came to write this poem because I was interested in weather at the time. I first started to write when I heard the musical version of The War of the Worlds *and Richard Burton's dramatic and haunting voice.'*

10

CHRISTOPHER SMITH

Aged 12
Loneliness

Loneliness is like being alive,
With everyone else dead.
A prisoner in a prison camp
Must feel like this at times.
A page without a book.
A man without his name.
The feelings of loneliness
Are nearly the same.
It feels as though a wave
Has covered you over.
So nobody can see where
You are or how you feel.
A cloud has come down
And hidden you from view
And nobody even cares
What's happening to you.

Christopher Smith is 15,
lives in Blyth, and goes to
Tynedale High School.
*'I dislike having to rush a
poem. I tend to change it
around a lot until it suits me,
so I usually take about an
hour of scribbling out. It was
my English teacher, Mr Allen,
who encouraged me to write
poetry at Bebside Middle School,
so I suppose he's my inspiration.'*

NEIL HENDERSON

Aged 10
Cold

Cold is the puppy with his wet soggy nose,
Cold as the crunchy, glistening snow
That sparkles on the garden path,
Snowmen, standing in the garden
With staring freezing eyes and carrot noses.
An icicle, crystal clear,
The sharp point frozen.
The lethal point that gives you a numbing,
Cold injection,
As cold as the top of a lemon meringue pie.

Neil Henderson is 11, lives
in Birtley, Co. Durham,
and is his school's football
captain. His poem was one
of a batch of impressive
poems sent in by Portobello
Primary School in Birtley.
*'Our topic for last winter was
"Cold". Our class all wrote a
poem and painted pictures. I
enjoy this part of my work
and have written several poems.'*

CHRIS LEATHLEY

Aged 12
Fear

I used to fear great heights.
Or being alone in darkness,
Locked, in a room,
With no way out.

As I walk along
A pair of eyes watch me,
They follow me intently,
Then I fall
Down a bottomless pit.

I fear the bomb,
The mushroom cloud,
The nuclear winter,
A very slow death.

Chris Leathley has moved up from Gosforth High School to Gosforth Central Middle. Now 13 and 'into soul music', he likes tropical geography and Spanish.

'My poem took about an hour to write (over two days!). I don't read a lot of poetry but a good friend of mine called Tom Pow recently had a book of poems published called Rough Seas. *I like some Ted Hughes and Roger McGough stuff.'*

DAVID MILLER

Aged 12
Stolen

I sit on a stool, head in hands,
Feet quaking at any thought.
I rush out into the garden,
My heart pounding, pounding.
Leaves quiver like feathers.
Twigs point, saying 'Guilty! Guilty!'

I can no longer take pain.
I have visions of agony.
How will I ever repent?
The soil crunches, giving me up
Five pence, that's all, five pence.
I'll have to confess, I'll have to confess.

David Miller is 12, and goes to Gosforth Central Middle School. He is a keen sportsman, but has always been good at English too.

'I wrote this poem in class. It was supposed to be about guilt.'

CATHERINE STRAW

Aged 10
The Winter Village

The winter village
Stands in the countryside.
Desolation and cold
Enter the dead land.

Market square, covered in snow,
Icicles hanging from the florist's,
Bread in the window of the baker's shop,
Butcher's meat rotting away.

A monument for the founder
With a frosted wreath beside.
It is now quiet,
Time has stopped.

Neat little cottages
All in a row,
A tiny park with a frozen stream,
A statue of the mayor.

A small churchyard
Stands cold and dead.
Into the church I step,
Ghostly music plays from the steeple.

Now I am leaving,
Back through the countryside.
Time starts again for me
But not for the winter village.

Catherine Straw is 10, lives in Whitley Bay and goes to La Sagesse Convent School in Newcastle.

'I wrote about winter because it is a season when time seems to have stopped. That is what I tried to say in the poem. I like poems of all sorts, but I enjoy reading Edward Lear's nonsense poems best of all. My father wrote a lot of poems for me when I was little (he still does) and that made me interested in writing my own poems.'

MELISSA GRAHAM

Melissa Graham comes from Sunderland, went to Houghton School, and is now spending a year in France as an au pair before going to university. This poem was written during a writers' course at Lumb Bank sponsored by Sunderland Education Authority.

'It was a difficult poem to write – I think mental illness is something people tend to shy away from, even when they know someone who is suffering from it. But Janni Howker, one of the writers in residence, was very sympathetic, understanding and encouraging – she told me not to be afraid of listening to my feelings and writing them down.'

Aged 17
Asylum

She sits and stares with hollow eyes at
Nothing. Blank, unmoving, vaguely wondering
      why she is
Like she is; a rag-bag of rambling emotions all
Falling apart at the seams.

The gaping dark that swallowed up her dreams
Stares back and seeps into her brain
Like a drug: a deep, dark drug dragging her
Down, dulling her tongue. Creeping through her
      veins

Like the valium they give her every morning
To take away the pain of
Living? Sleeping? Breathing?
But always too little. Never enough.

Still they leave a cruel shred, a grain
Of tortuous self-awareness,
Just enough to let her know
That she's insane.

JOANNE CHIPCHASE

Aged 14
Dying Day

An old man sleeps throughout the day,
The clock that ticks his life away.
Uneaten food upon the floor
Days have passed outside his door.
The day is short, the night is long,
He does not hear, will life drag on?
They do not know, nor do they care
That death is soon to linger there.

The old man turns upon his bed,
A pounding brain within his head.
His hands are cold, his flesh, it rots,
The temperature, it drops and drops.
His eyelids flutter, a rasping breath,
The room breathes in
Then death.

Joanne Chipchase did the parrot picture on the back cover of this book, and describes herself as 'a fun-loving 15 year old' and 'not quite the stereotype poet'. She is a pupil at Dame Allan's Girls School in Newcastle, where this poem was written during a chemistry lesson.

SARAH COX

Aged 16
The Painful Truth

There's a child in my throat, trying to get out,
If you listen quite closely, you might hear her shout –
'It's easy, you know, to stop all this pain;
If we give the food, he'll give the rain.'
She's an idealist, you see, one of the twits.
Green as they come and without all her wits.
I tell her it's useful, that these things take time,
But she says it's attitudes that caused all the crime.
I've asked her to stop; my throat is so sore,
But each time I swallow, she comes up for more.

Sarah Cox is 17, lives in Ponteland, and goes to Queen Elizabeth High School in Hexham.
'If I have a problem, or am concerned about something, a poem can clear my head quicker than some pill. The real me is the "child in my throat", and the poem is describing the desperate struggle kids' have against the argument and "wisdom" of adults.'

DAMIEN CHARLTON

Aged 10
I couldn't manage on my own

Damien Charlton is now
13, and goes to St Cuthbert's
High School in Newcastle.
He visited an old people's
home in Gosforth with St
Charles Roman Catholic
Primary School: *'When I
returned I tried to think of an
interesting way to write the
visit up, to write a poem was
the answer.'*

We went into this room,
Four old ladies sat there, silent,
Don't suppose they heard or saw us,
They just sat there.

'Mind if we ask some questions
For the Doomsday Project?' we asked.
'No,' came a crackly reply.
She loved the home!

Then we interviewed the owner.
'Ninety is the average age.
Between them they have lived
Two thousand one hundred
And sixty years.
Relatives are a big problem,' she said.
Old age is a problem, I thought

Ladies were here so their families
Could go on holiday,
Some have no relatives so they hardly ever get out.
But once they all went to Whitley Bay.
We asked one lady why she had decided to live here.
She said; 'Do you know I've never ridden
A bike before in my life?'
We tried again,
'I couldn't manage on my own,' she said,
And we all knew it was true.
'I couldn't manage on my own,' she said again.
'But my sons are doing very well.'

DANIEL MAIER

Aged 16
Valentine's Day

She pads down the stairs with an air of depression,
The imminent end of her yearly obsession.
She tiptoes, and cuddles the unconcerned cat,
And putting it down she kneels on the mat;
A faint rise of hope as she looks at each letter;
Picking them up, she should have known better;
Reluctantly sorting them, no one to blame,
She holds to her breasts the three in her name.
Gliding upstairs her expression is blank,
A note from the Post Office, one from the bank;
At the edge of her bed, nobody to hear,
On the last letter drops a solitary tear.
Joining last year's, up on the shelf,
The Valentine card she sent to herself.

Daniel Maier went to New-castle's Royal Grammar School, and is now studying English at Leeds University.

'I wrote Valentine's Day *for the school magazine. I usually find I dislike my poems shortly after I write them – but I still like this one.'*

CLARE NICHOLSON

Aged 10
My Uncle Martin

My Uncle Martin is such a bore,
He sits and talks and talks,
And whenever you want to go
He says 'No, please don't go.'
Then my mam doesn't have the heart
To leave him on his own.
So we sit for another half an hour
Until we lose our Strength and Power.
And then we end up sleeping
At my Uncle Martin's house.

Clare Nicholson is 10, lives at Rowlands Gill, and goes to St Joseph's Roman Catholic School at Rowlands Gill.

'I made my Uncle Martin up purely out of my own imagination. I have read more of Roald Dahl's stories than poems and I enjoy reading all kinds of stories.'

SARAH BARLOW

Sarah Barlow plays the flute and recorder, goes to ballet, tap, modern and disco classes, and wants to be a dancer. Now 13, she goes to Southlands County Middle School in Cramlington, but wrote the first of these poems as part of a school project at Cragside County First School.

'I wanted to show how it felt to be cold and lonely on the wall. I feel poetry should be a way of telling others your feelings without boring them. I dislike poems that are too abstract. Ted Hughes is my favourite poet. His poems often give me ideas for my own poems. I think that my own style of writing is like his. Most of the poetry I read is by the Elizabethan poets.'

'I wrote the dog poem in my English class for Hallowe'en. I wanted my poem to be something different because nearly all Hallowe'en poems are the same.'

'I wrote Destruction after listening to some poems that likened Autumn to a person. I used one of the boys in our class and exaggerated the character a bit (well a lot!!)'

Aged 9
The Roman Wall Blues

The damp misty air bites round my ankles,
On the bare spindly branches icicles hang.
The weary Romans tramp around the frosty field,
As night falls the blackened sky turns to wet,
Cold and pouring rain.
I pull my cloak tightly round my shoulders,
The tingling feel of ice cold is in my toes.

Aged 12
Who Walks the Dog?

In and out the rusty leaves
Round and round the groaning trees,
Through the puddles
Up the lane,
Over tree tops,
Down again.

Startled cats with golden eyes,
Staring into moonlit skies,
Dogs on broomsticks!
What a sight,
Enough to give a spook a fright.

Black shapes flutter round the moon,
A strange, a howling sort of tune,
As mum below is heard to cry,
'What's Rover doing in the sky?'

A crash, a thump,
Down to the ground
Bumps a rather startled hound.
Was that a walk, or trick or treat?
At least he ain't got muddy feet!

Aged 12
Destruction

Go!
Shouted the Autumn boy,
Throwing his stick in the air.
Go away you stuffy summer.
I am here
Yes, me!
AUTUMN
I have come
It is my turn.
I'll bring displeasure into the year.

I will carry my stick
All over town and country
And change your summer green leaves
To strong brown.
The time is mine
To do as I wish

Now, where shall I start?
Here with you, wise old tree,
You cannot stand up to me now,
I will pull your branches,
Tear your leaves and leave you,
Cold and bare for winter,
I shall make you suffer.

Do I hear someone laughing?
You, mighty sun?
Your turn will come.
You shall suffer also,
Your colour shall change from gold to orange,
Your days shall be shorter.
You laugh again?
You laugh at your peril.

Tomorrow I shall start,
On land and sea.
I shall run through gardens
Turning them inside out
I shall make my Autumn
A time to remember.

ALISON BAKER

Alison Baker is 17, lives in Heworth, and is now doing a social care course at North Tyneside College.

'The poem started with the first two lines one afternoon, when I suddenly remembered seeing large dragonflies one hot summer's day when I was about 7. The image is still very clear to me, the rest of the poem followed quickly.'

'My poetry is written from feelings and experiences. I dislike having a set subject to write about. Two of my favourite poets are Edgar Allan Poe and Frances Horovitz.'

Aged 17
Reason To Be

I am dragonfly,
I carry the sky on my wings.
Watch me, each spin, dart, turn,
Follow my sun dance.
I burn the light.

I am worm,
I wear the earth as a cloak.
Beneath is dark, warm, safe,
An intertwining labyrinth.
I leave this behind me.

I am dolphin,
I dream of sunlight on water,
See the rainbow sparkling, blinding,
Dazzling,
Dancing on the waves.
I live for this.

I am scorpion,
I stand alone in the fire.
Around me flames twist, taunt,
Devour,
Yet are as ice to me.
I remain in ascendancy.

SACHA ALLEN

Aged 12
Danger

Her neck arched up higher,
she dodged to the side.
No need to be scared,
just a feeling inside her.

His ears pricked up forward,
and his eyes opened wide.
A stamp with his hind foot
told the others to hide.

Something was hovering above her,
it was no friend and indeed no brother.
Filled with fear, horror and dismay,
as fast as she could she scurried away.

He's always listening for a particular sound,
the beating of hooves and a bark of a hound.
As soon as he hears this he gallops away,
for this is the game that no one should play.

Each animal at its adversary grins,
for death is the prize the enemy wins.

Sacha Allen, now 15, has moved up from Gosforth Central Middle School to Gosforth High.

Her poem *Danger* was inspired by Richard Adams's novel Watership Down: *'It described the animals' reactions to dangerous situations. Also at the time I had a pony, so I was very aware of how she reacted when she was frightened.'*

NICOLA BARTON

Nicola Barton is 12, lives in Burnopfield, and goes to Church High School in Newcastle. She has two cats, likes animals, and wants to be a vet.

'I had to write a poem at school about an animal, and chose to write about a tiger because it is my favourite breed of wild cat. My favourite poet is T.S. Eliot, especially his Old Possum's Book of Practical Cats.'

Aged 9
The Tiger

Prowling round the forest, in the dead of night,
Giving timid animals a dreadful fright.
Lying in the grasses, his eyes begin to gleam
And if you are about you're sure to hear a scream.
Stripy back and careful feet
The vicious tiger hunts his meat.
His tail bent low, his eyes begin to search
He spies a young antelope sleeping by a birch,
Up behind the birch tree he begins to creep.
All of a sudden he gives a mighty leap,
He hits the target, lands his prey
And drags it to a corner and begins to slay.
He gives a growl and takes a bite,
He tugs at the antelope with all his might.
And now I am sad to say
We'll never see that antelope again
Prancing on his way.

Aged 12
The Lesser Purple Emperor

Dusty purple, marbled pink,
Tender wings that flutter by.
The lavish flapping of the wings,
That grace both air and sky.
A lesser emperor though he be,
He still delights the eye,
His royal purple flowing robe
Flapping as he flies.

His furry body clothed within
A flowing cloak of purple silk.
He flies and lands on poplar trees,
To drink their sweetened milk.

22

His stunning body flows through the air
As he stoops down to drink.
He lands and folds his wings,
Of purple and of pink.

He's like a little aeroplane,
Buzzing through day and night.
He flies with grace with
Those wings coloured so bright,
And as he swishes through the darkness,
And flutters through the light,
All those who see him admit
He is a stunning sight.

RICHARD BUCKTON

Aged 9
Volcanoes! Volcanoes!

And lava.
They pour from the top
Like water dripping from a mop
It drips and it drops
It all comes from the top
Slirt splurt
Look at all the dirt
Bubbling boiling
And also spoiling.
Lava! Lava!
Coming down the mountain like whipped cream.
All of a sudden I heard a scream
A person burnt by the whipped cream.
I heard another scream
More chocolate and soda cream
More screams
Wait a minute! Look!
The chocolate and cream is
Now a vicious soda stream.

Richard Buckton lives in Monkseaton, Whitley Bay, goes to Monkseaton Middle Shool, and was at Monkseaton Village First School when he wrote Volcanoes at the age of 'nine nearly ten'. He was born in Wallsend, has lived in the Middle East and Asia, and is now 13.

'We were drawing pictures. I drew a Volcano, then I wrote the poem Volcanoes to go with the picture. I also like funny rhymes and silly poems.'

ISHITA SHABDE

Ishita Shabde comes from India, and is now 12. She has moved up from La Sagesse School to Central Newcastle High.

'My idea came from when I used to go for walks with my mother and she would exclaim about the magnificent colours in the late summer evenings. I think rhyming poems sound good but again I don't write much of that. My kind of poetry is descriptive.'

Aged 10
The Sky

The evening sky is beautiful
With pink orange and blue.
The colours blend with
Puffs of clouds which look like
White marshmallow.
Hour by hour the pale colours
Dissolve and disappear
And fade into blue light tinged with black.

The morning sky is a splendid sight,
The pale blue background and rising sun
Appear like a framed picture.
As afternoon comes the sun shines even brighter
And the blue turns a shade darker
Then the afternoon sky fades slowly into evening.

BETH FERNANDEZ

Beth Fernandez used to go to Newminster Middle School in Morpeth. She is now 15, and has moved to Bedfordshire.

'I think that unless the poet is exceptionally clever at rhyming you have more freedom with free verse, and it therefore comes out better in the poem.'

Aged 12
A Winter's Scene

A sleek black ribbon unwinds over the countryside
Interspersed with bundles of delicate white feathers
Speckled with brightly coloured mobile figures
Marred by the sight of mangled modern contraptions
Enlivened momentarily by a solitary bird's
                    seasonal tune
Depressed by the careless hum of the salt sprinkler
And flavoured by that indefinable quality of winter.

SATOKO HONDA

Aged 11
The Mountain

The mountain is big
Bigger than anything else

The mountain is a dandy
He always wears a hat of snow
And a jumper of snow

The mountain is shy
He hides his face with clouds

The mountain is naughty
He throws a huge snowball
At a mountaineer

The mountain is cold
If you go to the top of the mountain
You are in the freezer

But the mountain in spring
Is always very beautiful

Satoko Honda couldn't speak
a word of English when
she came to England at the
age of 9. She is now 12,
lives in Low Fell, and goes
to La Sagesse High School.
*'I was thinking about the title
of poem and I never wrote a
poem about the mountain be-
fore and I also remembered
about Japanese famous moun-
tain called Fuji and I thought
I could write about it.'*

CHRISTOPHER MORDUE

Christopher Mordue is 18, and comes from Durham. He went to Dame Allan's Boys School, and is now studying law at St John's College, Oxford.

'*I wrote* Barn Owl *after watching a natural history documentary. The "pity-drained heart" on the barn owl's face is an attempt to explain why a feature associated with love should appear on the face of such a ruthless killer.*'

'*Originally,* Seasons *consisted only of the final stanza. The idea came from seeing bare trees in a winter landscape, and thinking that they looked like agonised, twisted hands.*'

'*The inspiraton for* The Only End of Age *came from Philip Larkin's poem* Dockery and Son *in which Larkin spells out his view of life as empty and final.*'

Aged 16
Barn Owl

Dusk, and the sun is swallowed
In the hole it burnt for itself in the hill top.
The world stands blackened, funereal.
Charred trees mark the sun's descent –
They smoulder gently, making this thin mist
Which spirals, as a momentary breeze
Trembles the forest floor altar.

Gleaming, the white shadow of a barn owl
Ghosts through the columned stumps,
Padding on rubber-soled wings,
Silently tearing the thin mist-veil
With muscle-filled wingbeats.

This forest is his kingdom –
He knows every dry-leaved wind-rustle,
And every scurrying panic of his subjects.
Here, his screech is the only Word
And God is his air-solidifying death-drop.

Mercy is not in his vocabulary –
He needs no love or pity in his life,
(Long ago, he thrust his beak through Love –
Now he wears the pity-drained heart on his face).

With infinite patience, he hunts the fear below.
But the moment to unleash his body, arrow-like,
Towards the mortal squeak, is future-time.
For now, he waits.

Aged 16
Seasons

I

Just when the world thought it was dead,
The sun came back over the hills like the 7th Cavalry,
The clock skipped an hour, chiming the Resurrection,
And the world decided to take another chance,
To try to make something permanent this time,
And the tree's buds bulged towards May.

II

The sun hung huge above the world
Laid out on a slab of blue marble,
Paralysed by the heat,
While man cowered in the shade,
Or, prostrate, offered up his body to be burnt.

III

Season of decay and growing darkness!
It rained leaves, everywhere was covered
In a deep, rotting, stinking brown.
The world crunched underfoot, and all turned black,
Or crawled into a grave to outsleep Death.

IV

It was like the aftermath of some great fire –
The earth stood knee-deep in ashes,
And December squeezed tighter on the world,
Until only the dead's charred hands strained higher,
Begging to a distant sun for mercy.

Aged 16
The Only End of Age

Looking down from the sunset
He could see that all the sand
Had slipped between his fingers
Into the pool below.
And now his hands were empty.

And as he tried to take stock
Of the last few grains still clinging
To his open palm, he could see,
Between his parted fingers,
His face reflected in the empty blue water.

And a sudden image flashed across his mind
Of a man falling from a mountain top,
Who, sensing death, turns his face to the summit
To see how far he has fallen, how long he has left,
But sees only the empty nothingness of sky.

And so he pulled his deckchair to the water's edge,
And sat down to enjoy the last eyeful of light
From the dying embers of a dying sun.

PAUL THOMPSON

Aged 8
God of Thunder and Lightning

I am the God of thunder and lightning
My name is Thunderflash
I slice trees in half
I set the wood alight
I light up the sky on dark nights
People think I am frightening
People say it is God walking
I blow holes in the ground.

Aged 8
Morning

Hello Moon
It's nearly morning
You'd better run.
Oh no Moon
Here comes the sun
You've no time to run.

Paul Thompson is 9, lives in Chopwell, and goes to Chopwell Junior School. He likes all sports, especially American football.

'God of Thunder and Lightning *is the first poem I have written. We were asked at school by our headmaster Mr Meegan to write a poem for the competition. These poems are the only ones I've written.*'

EDWARD PICKETT

Edward Pickett is 12, lives in Blakelaw in Newcastle, and has moved up from English Martyrs Primary School to St Cuthbert's.

'I have only one hand. I have a bionic hand. I play football for Montagu football club. I have played for Newcastle boys and I'm rather proud of myself.'

'My poem is rather silly but I love it. I like poetry that rhymes but I write poems that don't rhyme. I love Pam Ayres, her poems are brilliant.'

Aged 9
The Frog and His Friends

There was once a Frog whose home was in a bog.
He had a friend called Tea whose home was in the
sea.
He had a friend called Jake whose home was in
the lake.
He had a friend called Beam who lived in the
stream.
He had a friend called Quiver who lived in a river.
One day they had a game of snooker,
And discovered a game of croak.
And the one that croaked the most was the
winner,
And named Skinner.

HENRY KIPPIN

Henry Kippin is 8, goes to Kelvin Grove Junior School in Gateshead. This poem was written in class at Wingrove Junior School.

'I don't like poetry that does not rhyme. A.A. Milne is my favourite poet.'

Aged 6
Eggs

I do not like the way you slide,
I do not like your soft inside,
I do not like your many ways,
And I can do for many days
Without eggs.

LEANNE CARNEY

Aged 9
Friends of Michael

I know a chimp called Michael the monkey
Who wears a stripy jumper,
You will find him running through the streets
In sunny Kuala Lumpa.

He has a penpal called Zularsu,
Who is an Indian elephant,
Zularsu lives in Timbuctoo
But that of course is totally irrelevant.

Another friend is called Ben,
Who has a brother called Len,
Neither gets up till ten
And as lions both lie straight down again.

Danny the donkey lives down our street,
He's had a lot of trouble with his feet,
With carrying people large and small,
Also giraffes which are very tall.

Michael's friends are many and far,
Including bears brown and polar,
Not forgetting Tiger and Carrot,
A rather strange name for a colourless parrot,
They are a weird and wonderful bunch,
I'll have to close it's time for lunch.

Leanne Carney lives in Washington, where she has her own pony. Now 12, she has moved up from La Sagesse Junior School to Dame Allan's Girls School in Newcastle.

'It was my mother's birthday and she was given a card with a number of cartoon characters on the front, that is how I came to write this poem.'

IAN CROZIER

Aged 9
My Pet

I have a pet,
He is my friend,
He has a head at the front
And a tail at the end.

He has pointed ears
And big brown eyes,
A thick furry coat,
And is quite a size.

For breakfast he has porridge,
For dinner he has meat,
And when he's been a good boy
Gets chocolate as a treat.

He runs around the garden,
He has his own football,
Does everything I tell him,
And comes when I call.

He has to have his exercise,
In sunshine, snow or fog.
Have you guessed yet what he is?
Of course he is my dog.

Ian Crozier is 12, and plays football for St Cuthbert's High School and for Montagu and North Fenham Boys Club in Newcastle. His teacher at English Martyrs Primary School heard about the Chronicle competition:

'Mr Ewart set the class the project of writing a poem. I thought that I would prefer to write about something I knew and I chose to write a poem about my dog Rebel.'

MICHELLE STACEY

Aged 9
I am a herring

I am a herring, a very funny herring,
I dance and sing and do all sorts of other things,
I do comedy shows to entertain my friends,
and now I am a very famous herring.

Michelle Stacey is 9, lives in Wallsend, and wrote her herring poem as part of a project at Richardson Dees First School.

'I have just started at Western Middle School. I love poetry and we all learned The North Ship *by Philip Larkin for the North Shields Fishing Festival.'*

32

NICHOLAS TELFORD-REED

Aged 12
My Mum's Mini

My mum's mini is fun, but old,
It's full of miles (and full of holes!)
The windows rattle, the bearings squeak,
While from the engine, fluids leak.

My mum's mini was once dull red,
But now it's only dull, instead!
The rust is creeping up the door,
(And possibly beneath the floor!)

My mum's mini used to roar
At eighty miles an hour or more.
But now it roars at fifty-four,
With mother's foot down to the floor!

My mum's mini is her best friend,
It's carried her for miles on end.
She thinks that she is Stirling Moss
And teaching's gain is racing's loss!

My mum's mini is hard to beat,
It's a "mean machine" while on the street.
And while its time is running out,
Its memory will live without a doubt!

Nicholas Telford-Reed lives in Whickham, and likes mountaineering, role-playing games and Manchester United. Now 14, he goes to the Royal Grammar School in Newcastle.

'The poem was written for English homework. Writing poetry is very hard work.'

DAVID ROUNTREE

Aged 8
Life as a herring

Being a herring is cold
and wet and dangerous
because we are fished
for. It's a hard job
dodging the nets.

David Rountree is 8, lives in Wallsend, and has a dog called Henry 'who likes to jump up and down'. His herring poem is another contribution from the Richardson Dees fishing project.

LINDSAY ARMSTRONG

Lindsay Armstrong is 10, lives in Howdon, and goes to Stephenson Memorial Middle School at Willington Quay, Wallsend. She collects pencil sharpeners.

'I like to write poetry and stories and when I saw this competition I decided to enter. I particularly like funny poems and enjoy poems and stories by Roald Dahl.'

Aged 10

Mr Redhead

Mr Redhead had awfully long ears.
One morning he woke up and broke out in tears
To find his ears at the bottom of his bed.
His ears must have grown from the top of his head.

Oh no what could have gone wrong?
How can my ears have grown so long?
Mr Redhead thought and thought:
What disease could I have caught?

My poor ears, said Mr Redhead,
How could they have reached the foot of my bed?
Mr Redhead bit the dust at the age of a hundred
        and seven.
Mr Redhead and his ears both went up to heaven.

HANNAH BAYMAN

Hannah Bayman is 10, goes to West Jesmond Junior School, and enjoys *'music, netball, writing, reading and stamp-collecting as well as poetry.'*

'I like all poems by Roald Dahl and another favourite is Spike Milligan.'

Aged 10

Mr Nobody

He leaves on lights all through the house,
Dropping crumbs on the sitting-room floor,
Making muddy marks,
Leaving an open door.
It's not us who spills the milk you see
But Mr Nobody.

EMMA REID

Aged 9
Bossy Parrot (My Sister)

Mum said, PIANO! Emma,
    Bossy Parrot said, Mum said piano!

Mum said, BATH! Emma,
    Bossy Parrot said, Mum said bath!

Mum said, SUPPER! Emma,
    Bossy Parrot said, Mum said supper!

That does it, I said.
Homework!! Move your blazer!
Move your bag!
My sister is a Bossy Parrot!!!

Emma Reid is now 11, and has moved up from West Jesmond Junior School to Gosforth Central Middle.

'I wrote Bossy Parrot *because I am the youngest in the family. I like poetry quite a lot because it explains very well what is happening. One of my favourite poets is Michael Rosen, because of the sort of poems he writes, and also reading his poems gives me good ideas of poems that I could write.'*

FIONA BOLAM

Fiona Bolam recites poetry at festivals. Now 10, she lives in Blaydon, and goes to Blaydon West Primary School.

'I like humorous poems like Matilda *by Hilaire Belloc. I wrote the Skeletor poem after watching my brother playing with He-man figures. The Steve Cram poem was written for our Sports Day programme.'*

'I enjoyed the Tam O'Shanter story when we saw the carvings of it in the Joicey Museum. We also went to see the Brig O'Doon and the old church at Alloway.'

Aged 7
Skeletor fled

Skeletor fled, and banged his head.
Tri-clops squeaked, with an eek, eek eek.
BUT up jumped Beast Man, and cracked his whip,
And the monster slipped on an apple pip.

Aged 7
Steve Cram pushes a pram

Steve Cram pushes a pram.
Steve Ovett sat on his pet.
Sebastian Coe dropped a hammer on his toe.
Mike McLeod talks very loud.

Aged 9
Tam O'Shanter

'I'm going to the pub
Can I have a sub?'
'You never take me out for some bait,'
Said Kate.

He got on his horse.
'You'll be careful of course.
The witches might get you
And cook you in a stew.'

'Don't be silly
You silly Billy
They won't get me.
Hee hee hee.'

He rode away to Ayr
To see his friends there.
And said will you come for a drink.
They said yes I think.

Could we have some beer?
Is it very dear?
Suddenly a storm blew up
'Awoo' said a little pup.

Let's have one last song.
It won't take very long.
Come on onto Grey Meg.
Oh you've cut your leg.

Away he went in the rain,
He sang to himself again.
He held tight onto his hat.
He thought he saw a witch's cat.

He thought what Kate had said.
He'd rather be in bed.
He saw the church ablaze with light.
So bright Tam nearly blinded his sight.

He saw some horrid witches
With their faces so nasty.
He thought that they reminded him
Of school dinner pasty.

They were so horrid
He felt he'd be sick.
He said 'Fetch a basin
Quick. Quick. Quick.'

He saw a lovely witch called Cutty Sark,
Her voice was like a sweet skylark.
He shouted 'Well done Cutty Sark'.
Then the other witches began to bark.

He rode away across the river.
When the witches saw it they began to shiver.
Cutty Sark grabbed hold of the horse's tail,
The horse let out a great loud wail.

ALEXANDER BOLAM

Aged 6
Oor Wullie

There's a wee wee scamp and he trails about,
With Murdoch on his tail.
His name is Oor Wullie, and he
Sits upon a pail.

He rides about on his cartie
And he hardly ever gets a party,
Cos he's naughty, that's why.

Alexander Bolam is Fiona Bolam's brother. Aged 6, he also goes to Blaydon West Primary School, and has won poetry reciting competitions at Stockton, Darlington and Ryton festivals. He likes cartoons:

'Our Dad reads us Oor Wullie stories every Sunday. I collect all the annuals, and also the Broons.'

MELANIE GUTHRIE

Aged 13
Teddy Boy

The sound of his crepe-soled shoes
was worse than the Nine O'Clock News.
His hair, flicked back with oil,
as neat as unused foil.
He squashed himself into
drainpipe trousers and, with his
bootlace tie, looked as
smart as a fly!

Melanie Guthrie is 12, lives in Dunston. Her poem was written in class at Dunston Comprehensive School.

'The English set I was in last year was reading Nigel Hinton's novel Buddy. We were asked to compose a poem about Terry Clark, a middle-aged teddy boy, who was Buddy's dad.'

JUSTINE BESSFORD

Aged 11
The Spider

The spider crawls along the hall,
On the ground and on the wall,
With hairy body and stick-like legs
And feet that look like washing pegs.

He looks around with tiny eyes
And gives a fly a slight surprise.
He opens his mouth like sliding doors,
Grabs the fly and shuts his jaws.

Now happy with his Sunday lunch,
He makes his way round to some flowers
    (a bunch),
He looks around for moths and flies
And sees his tea will be a prize!

He sees the grubs all squirming round
And licks his lips without a sound.
He eats a grub and crawls away.
Goodbye, spider for another day.

Justine Bessford is now 13.
She lives in Whickham and
goes to Central High School
in Newcastle. She has two
rabbits, two Siamese cats
and a terrapin, likes writing
funny poems and reading
Pam Ayres.

*'I was just feeling rather bored
so, as a means of doing some-
thing, I wrote a poem.'* This
was *The Spider*. Her other
poem, *Nonsense*, was done
for English homework.

*'I often find it difficult to
understand non-rhyming poems,
but am trying to tackle that
problem.'*

Aged 12 –
Nonsense

I was walking to the grocer's with me basket on me arm,
When I met the local vicar who was reading out a psalm.
I stopped to say good morning in the way that people do,
When a squeaky voice behind me yelled out very clearly 'BOO!'
Well, I thought this very strange so I turned around and looked
And there I saw a bumble bee well and truly hooked,
He was in the air and buzzing with a look of great despair,
He looked up at the black thing flying in the air,
He said it was a monster, I said I disagreed,
It looked more like a jellyfish tangled up in weed,
He looked at me with anger, and turned as if to go,
But I told him very smartly that I really did not know.

39

LUCY ROGERS

Lucy Rogers lives in
Sunderland, and goes to
Central Newcastle High
School. Now 16, she wrote
her poem in a car park.
*'I like reading Sylvia Plath
and Roger McGough; I quite
like Fleur Adcock. Listening to
Shostakovich's music helps me
to write poetry; the Beatles
also inspire me. I like cats
and water lilies. I am
inwardly composed but
outwardly disorganised.'*

Aged 15
Mother listening to Beatles tape in the car

She's heard this song so many times
It doesn't touch her any more;

It doesn't remind her of that other time,
When her hair flew around her
Instead of being clipped into salon neatness;
'Long hair was such a nuisance,'
She says, longing for it.

It can't disguise the noise of children
Buzzing around behind her like wasps,
Laughing like gaolers;

It can't take the wedding-chain from her finger.

And anyway,
    Ringo's drumbeats are giving her a headache.

So she turns off the youthful summer music,
And waits for her husband to come back from the bank.

KIRSTY MAYES

Aged 17
Hotel Eyes

Anyone can see
The red neon light
In her eyes,
Driven by the light
From her jar of medicine.
Pillar-box red lips.
All those hunting her,
Stalking, tracking
Her down need look
No further,
For she is here –
Vacancy, she has
Hotel Eyes.

Aged 17
Rising Like Fire

Rising like
Soft heat from
The furnace of night,
The mists are taken.
Swallowed,
Ready to be blown into
Action for another.
The sands travelling
With it, caught up
In all heat and
The passion.
Crawling across the crusts
Of earth
Like a convict who comes
Each day,
Not to make us afraid
But just to remind us.

Kirsty Mayes is 17, lives in Seaton Sluice, and is studying for her 'A' levels at Astley High School in Seaton Delaval. She won the Bloodaxe-sponsored Arvon course in the 1987 Chronicle competition.

'I write poems as a kind of diary so that I can remember what I have seen and how I saw it. Hotel Eyes *was written after a party I went to.'*

*'*Rising Like Fire *was originally written for another competition, one about water. When I was writing it I had the image of the beginning of* Great Expectations *in my head – hence the convict coming each day not to scare us.'*

IAIN PIGG

Iain Pigg lives in Dipton, Co. Durham. Now 17, he is studying for his 'A' levels at St Bede's School in Lanchester.

His *Poem Unwritten* is about why people "choose" to write poems: '*My musings on the matter being inconclusive, I decided that the poem must be something imposed on the author.*'

Thunderstorms can be explained, but Iain still feels awe when watching them. He calls his poem *Storm* a 'gentle protest': '*Ancient cultures had a god of some importance who was accredited with thunderstorms – gods such as Thor and Jupiter – and it seems a shame that modern technocrats should get away with outraging these gods, by explaining their secrets.*'

Aged 15
Poem Unwritten

There is a poem deep inside of me,
Wrenching to be out,
And if it isn't pouring from my fingertips
Like blood from a wound,
It is beating me, wanting to be born.

Some god has planted this brute in me.
It has been set to cudgel me
Until it can escape.
This poem is a dominating monster,
It is unnatural, and every birth
Deforms me.

Even when I have slaved
To scribble it across a page,
It laughs at me.

Aged 15
Storm

It is raining.
People are drowning
In the splashing rush
To find shelter.
The clouds are rising
Against the earth,
Laughing with silver tongues,
And screaming their distress.

Of course, any kid can bang
On a tin sheet to sound important.
Any god can drop a lighted match
Or a pair of scissors,

But the reality when the cutlery drawer
Is dropped on top of you:
That is the exclamation mark which
Ends the world . . .

HEIDI DOUGLAS

Aged 17
Birthday Girls

Birthday girls coming of age,
Lipstick stained, dry and bittersweet,
Bled red varicose, surround her lips.
Powdered eyes, thick, black and clotted.
Uncleansed from the fountains of youth.
Baptised by sweet cider and black.
Rolls, scrambling in cool sheets,
Half dressed, half naked.
Birthday girls coming of age,
Passing an annual initiation test.
Juices keep flowing till bile's revealed,
The more the better, more the braver.
Jukebox pumping chanted incantations.
Beds of ash scattered on powder pink carpets.
Stilettos bend under weighted oscillating bodies.
Heavy heads lift from feathered pillows.
Coming around, desired waters to satisfy
A youthful thirst.
Her fountain all ran dry.
Birthday girls coming of age.

Heidi Douglas is 18, and lives in Newcastle, and is one half of a two-woman drama group called Newton's Cradle.

'I wrote the poem after seeing a group of underage girls drunk in the Bigg Market one Saturday night, tottering around on really high heels and giggling.'

NICOLA WALKER

Nicola Walker is 18, and
now studying at Monkwear-
mouth College of Higher
Education. She lives in
Washington, and used to
go to Washington School.
The poets she admires range
from Shakespeare, Shelley,
Owen and Auden to con-
temporary poets like Fleur
Adcock and Douglas Dunn.
She wrote *Poison* while on
a writers' course at Lumb
Bank.

'After reading The Bell Jar *by
Sylvia Plath, I felt that my
poetry changed. I began to
write about very personal things,
but in an obscure and abstract
way. The cat poem is about
discovering the truth – about
yourself and others.'*

Aged 17
Poison

I could feel it,
Bubbling under my surface for a long time.
It was waiting until it had all its reserves prepared,
All standing by,
Ready for the word of their head.
I anticipated its arrival,
But there was nothing that could be done to stop
       it coming.
The irreversible process was beginning.
And I could just sit and wait.

And I did wait.
And it did come. Eventually.
But there was no way I could have been ready for
       its size:
It overwhelmed my life force,
And subdued my personality.

I lived with this shaming beast for an age;
Then it vanished.
It left no traces, but remained a vital reminder
Of my self-disgust,
And the loathsome taunts of "friends",
At this malformed entity
That forced its way into my body
Without an invitation.

Aged 17
The next day, someone ate the cat

The next day, someone ate the cat. And
Mother baked a cake; and father attempted
Suicide again; and I hit the girl who
Told me the truth about myself.

I hit her with a pick-axe. Or a sledge-
Hammer, I forget. I would have liked to
Have done it again, had she still been
Alive; and had it not been the truth.

Mother's cake sank in the middle. As
Always. And father failed to die. This is
Because he always forgets something. Like
The fact that he can swim, and breathe; and
Can know the truth.

I wonder about the cat. If it felt
Alive as it was eaten, or if it just lay
There and pretended death as it died. And
If it knew that one day, everyone would
Know the truth!

ELAINE CUSACK

Elaine Cusack is 17, lives in Felling, and goes to Church High School in Newcastle. After winning a Bloodaxe-sponsored Arvon course in the 1985 Chronicle competition, she published a pamphlet of poems called *Breakfast with Lydia Lunch*. She now gives readings, has appeared on TV on *Blockbusters*, and has just won the Athena Children's Prize for 1987. She lists her influences as Sylvia Plath, Philip Larkin, and songs with 'ideologically sound' lyrics, especially jazz, gospel and African music, and the Smiths.

'The Tenerife poem is tightly written, and each stanza focusses on a different aspect of the island. Attitude etc *was sparked off by an old man I visit regularly. He is 84 and refuelled my belief in God (along with the help of the ideas of the Housemartins). He showed me that Christianity is pure socialism.'*

Aged 15
Housewife am I

You've ruled my life since the age of nought,
And expect a ruler's wage.
But what is there to give?
You did the expected,
That unwritten law.

I curl up and sleep for millions of minutes,
With my head on your bedroom floor.
Housedust flies up my holes and through my
          system,
Yet my lungs continue to work.
Books keep my eyes from snapping shut,
But your bookscase is the goal I'll never achieve.
Your perfect life tugs at my greed.

You left our "home" before I returned,
And I have not seen you for weeks.
Tomorrow you'll arrive armed with apologies:
You must not expect your sweet tea in bed –
But your manhood on the mat.

Aged 15
You're handsome but hopeless

You're handsome but hopeless.
We have nothing in common.
Your incessant mauling made me frigid
(Bored me rigid)
I'd rather die than go to bed with you.

Aged 15
Missionary in El Salvador

Oh this wretched room, crammed with material things.
She, this saint owned my room,
Sinning came easier than the good:
But she took responsibilities and the other world called.
She went, and this made her special;
The voice of those deemed to be mute.

They did not want her for she was a helper,
And it took a death to mark their mood.
Tears because she could have stopped it.
(In reality nothing ceases bullet-fire.)

And did it hurt?
I should think so,
Yet I doubt that she cared;
For her mind was fixed on skin against dirt,
And bare soles on the bloodstained floor.

Aged 15
The Royal Grammar School, Newcastle

The R.G.S. make me sick.
They wear a black uniform, from the third year on;
In the sixth form they change to grey.
Then they leave and join a bank.

Aged 16
Short thought

I wish I had rings running through me like trees,
Then you'd know I wasn't lying about my age.

Aged 16
Blood relative

You crept in
I winced
I faked
You continued.

Sometimes I wished I could slap on a mask,
Peel it off and find another underneath
Or even scrape at the scum:
But the guilt I never wanted,
I just couldn't wipe away.

I became obese,
But you wanted me all the more.
I didn't wash,
So my outside matched the grime within:
I wanted to be noticed.

You found out,
This was a trust betrayed:
So you showed me 'the only way' –
I hid my feelings
And your greatest fear.

Aged 16
She's stuck to my formica breakfast bar

Grief is like guilt –
If it's left to simmer with its lid on,
It thickens, boils over
And leaves indelible stains.

That's why it's best to drag it out into the open
Because it's not shameful
Or one big secret
Like guilt can be.

I believe grief can be shared:
Just like good chocolate should be
And most schoolbooks have to be.

Aged 17
Such a thing

You look like a shorn lamb with that turnip haircut;
I bet you've got more hair on your legs
Even though you're a girl.
Tonight, however, it doesn't matter
Because we can *see* you're a girl.

You're wearing one of your well-known dresses,
Bought from that second-hand shop:
I know, for I was with you that day.
You always loved to browse, didn't you?
And you queued to go into jumble sales.

Yes, tonight you're at your best.
Music, that security blanket you cling to
Isn't here.
You say you don't need it
But you still look exposed to me.

Tonight you're a girl;
You attract them
And they flatter you.
You are admired,
How they love you!

But tonight I was the only one,
The others didn't notice;
They couldn't think of such a thing,
Not even that poet who follows you everywhere,
HE couldn't dream up such a story.

They haven't seen the symptoms yet;
You hide the tiredness with your smile,
You ignore the pins and needles
And you've only fainted twice.

So I wonder,
As you dance for them on the tabletops
And they cover you in orchids;
When will they see it can happen to anyone
And that there's no hope for their young hopeful.

Aged 17
Tourism is the major industry in Tenerife

On this island
Where the grass is as brittle as burnt wicks
And cats' lives are as easily snapped by vehicle wheels,
I plan to spend a fortnight.

On the balcony
I offer myself up to the sun
And like all meat, I'm burnt.
I sacrificed my wage to be sacrificed.

This strange fruit
Is wondrous and its name, unpronounceable.
It's the sort I've only stared at
In Marks and Spencer foodhalls

The small shrines
At the roadside worry me.
My driver hates his seat belt
And I've known people who've been killed "abroad".

The northern village
Contrasts with luxury holiday homes
Built by, amongst others, northern villagers.
Building contractors' annual turnovers, treble.

At the harbour
The meal reminds me of another we shared.
Swigging wine, lukewarm with heat
Looks so bohemian with bread and cheese!

The sea of course never changes
But it's warmer than Tynemouth
And sea salt, I think tastes better
Than morning tea that blots out the night before.

Aged 17
Attitude, as in positive: Reason, the ability to use our acquired knowledge

If you've got any half-baked romantic ideas
From newspapers, television, your mother
Or whatever,
That anyone here has the faintest idea where the hell they are going,
Or is sure of a single thing,
Then just go over and talk to someone.
Spend some time with that person:
You will find contradictions, unpaid bills, a messy kitchen,
And you will soon discover
That people don't always have intercourse when they sleep together;
It's not like the films you know.

There's this person I know who I often visit
And when I go we talk for hours;
I wish everyone could hear what he says.
I write it down so it won't be forgotten
But it's not the same as hearing *him* speak the words:
He could win any argument hands down.

Do you know
That this man has made me realise
That Attitude and Reason are the only things
You should allow to take up
Great lengths of your time and thoughts?
I know no one's perfect
But they can try
And I will personally hand out prizes for effort:
We can hold the prize-giving ceremony at my house if you want.

COLLEEN PRENDERGAST

Colleen Prendergast lives in North Shields, and was 'brought up on John Donne, Shakespeare and Marlowe'. She won first prize in 1984 when she went to Collingwood Primary School, and has now won prizes in the Chronicle competition for four years running. Now 14, and a pupil at Norham High School, she collects unicorns, and likes writing, pizzas and going to the theatre.

Band of Hope was inspired by the Jarrow March: 'I decided to write a poem which would show my feelings about my working-class area and the history of the North-East.'

'I like find nature programmes very interesting, and I think Flight *echoes the balance of nature, with the hunter and hunted each playing their part.'*

'Night was written at school, in English. After casting around for something to write about, I got a very clear image of a girl waiting for a date who didn't arrive. It's rather sad, but I think it's also quite true, human beings are quite blinkered when it comes to love.'

Aged 11
The Unicorn

Snow, silent, whispering down,
Coating the trees with lacy silk.
And through the pure white soundless blanket
Comes a horse as white as milk.
Its eyes are soft and ice-like blue.
It swishes its pure white silken tail,
It bears an icicle on its forehead.
Hard and pure like drops of hail,
It's crystal clear and proudly borne,
Daintily stepping through the forest
Among the snow lives a unicorn.

Aged 11
Winter's Family

Winter is a huntsman,
And Ice is his daughter,
Clothed in a gown
Of lace made of water.
Her necklace is an icicle,
All prisms of light,
She hangs these frozen dewdrops
On trees at night.
Snow is his lady,
All softly she falls,
Making the trees
Into white marble halls.
Frost is his son,
He clings to the walls,
Painting them silver,
Afraid lest he falls.
They sit on their thrones,
All coated in white,
But soon they are gone,
They have fled with the night.

Aged 12
Flight

Eagle: A clear sweet breeze is drifting by; although a pleasant thing
        My eagle's craggy feathers sigh to drift on prayer and wing.
Mouse: The grass is tall, and hides me too, a shivering tiny wreck,
        Who scans the vast unclouded blue for an evil, waiting speck.
Eagle: At last this breeze is good and strong, and I can arch my back.
        Although my wait was far too long, no power now I lack.
Mouse: And now he comes, the evil one, with shadow-beating wings,
        A silhouette, who, sparing none, of black deaths' praises sings.
Eagle: I glide on air, backwing to snatch, and spread my talons wide.
        To gather up a twitching patch; a rodent, terrified.
Mouse: The wings of death are swooping near, and hypnotised, I stare
        At glinting plumes of pain and fear, and talons as they tear.
Eagle: The sky above, a deep rich blue, parts into two for me.
        I, and the creature that I slew, glide regal, proud and free.

Aged 13
Band of Hope

The children of a 'murdered town'
Kissed their fathers, wished them well.
Those Jarrow men of great renown
Marched to still the funeral knell.

Crusading for the chance to work,
That basic right to them denied,
Bishops, crusaders for the church,
This, their heartfelt cause decried.

Their money came from clothes in pawn.
They marched to rise up from the murk.
Their meagre 'dole' was then withdrawn.
They 'weren't available for work'.

'Red Ellen', M.P. with the band,
Stole a march on parliament,
Which hid in lies for 'future plans'
And promised jobs they never sent.

Aged 13
Night

Waiting in a corner, in the silence, in the rain,
For the high, sharp sound of footsteps coming near,
A pool of light bars closing night,
And glistening streets reflect her brimming tears.

Heart lifting as a figure hurries down the rainwashed pavement,
Down a frozen midnight river, hollow, chill,
Her hope is vain, belief insane,
But faith in what he's promised holds her still.

At last the truth is realised and the corner is deserted,
A solitary figure walks away.
This spot she haunts, still pale and gaunt,
For a ghost that no one ever thought to lay.

Aged 14
Evacuation

All-clear sounding through dust and fire,
Bedroom wall exposed to the neighbours,
The damp patch Mam was so ashamed of, peeling away,
Teddy with his arm hanging limp
And his head blasted off.
A white hand sticking through the rubble
From The Safe Place Under The Stairs.
Adult eyes flickering away from a steady gaze.
Parcelled up at the station,
Tagged with a scrawled label like an unwanted Christmas gift.
Not allowed to stay at home,
Being punished for a crime so dreadful
It was unspeakable.
Sent to an old lady who hated noise
And couldn't be bothered with small children.
Sitting alone before a glass-panelled door
With dust-motes swirling lazily
In red and blue tinted light.
40 years on, left with a horror of stained glass
And the men called Winston and Adolf.

Aged 14
View from the Classroom Window

Wire mesh criss-crossing the outside world,
Wooden fence fallen, dipping and rising in a frozen wave,
Small, fat bird pecks the bubble-gum freckled ground,
Splintered lolly sticks spattered across the deserted yard,
Staunch green poles stretching out the diamond-patterned wire
Across the houses' blue-washed slates.
Hydrangeas spilling over a warm-red wall in a profusion of lilac and pink
Stipple-tinted blue.
Grass sloping down from the green field,
Rusted, hinged gates flung open.
Warped window-ledge,
Faded black pen, ghost-words on brown paint-work:
        Lisa L-v-S Stephen
            Liar
          L i a r
         L I A R

KIRSTY WHITEHEAD

Kirsty Whitehead was 15
when she started writing
poetry. In 1986, while at
Central Newcastle High
School, she won the Athena
Children's Prize in the com-
petition, as well as the
Bloodaxe-sponsored Arvon
course. Now 18, and study-
ing English at Magdalen
College, Oxford, she has
just won 3rd prize in the
Young Observer children's
poetry competition and
another Arvon course in
the adult section of the
Chronicle competition.
*'I try to jolt people in my
poems, to say something diffe-
rent from what they expect to
hear. In Daisies I was experi-
menting with colloquial or
casual forms of speech, and
also illustrating my vision of
nature as something powerful
and potentially dangerous,
rather than domesticated.'*

Aged 18
Homily

I am tissue paper thin,
shining like rain
and angry.
This is the third time
that God has not answered me.
I am fractious.

Behold me at the transept
early in the morning,
as white and ready to be
holy
as bottled milk.
I am touchstone, I am
tinderbox. I will strike
my prayers off flint
and make them fly upwards –
I may have to push with
both hands.
I am holy milk, I am
trying to be good.

But you, robust pink stones –
just like the fathers,
with the dimples pressed into your cheeks
by an awareness of latent salt water.
You tell me nothing.
I have come here looking
for cordial,
and you tell me nothing.

There is nothing. Nothing but
skeletal sunlight,
tapping its death certificate on
the priory gate.

Aged 17
Daisies

Life in the metropolis
Is just a load of laughs:
From the mushroom-pated businessmen on the Metro
To the breakfast lady and her convoy of dirty Irish jokes,
I love 'em all.

Daisies have been rising lately,
Bursting from their roots and sprouting all over the city.
The bus drivers looked a little disconcerted at first,
Then they laughed – and left a tyre load of daisies decapitated.
Schuh is knee-deep in daisies
(or should I say daisy deep)
They're serving them for lunch at the 'Farmhouse';
Wrapped in pastry.

Rodents though
            That's the problem
                        You can't keep those damn plants free
So they had the insecticide helicopter over,
And everything's sticky to the touch –
Thin and shiny, rather beautiful really;
Like the cellophane covering of a new book – WE LOOK.
Yes, we were there too at the time,
Daisying away.
The helicopter took us with them.
Those who swallowed the sticky substance died,
And we buried them down among the daisies.

Aged 17
Deer at Dawn

I can't remember much of it now.
Only the ragged vine branches –
Mad and beautiful, like old women
Abandoning their sterility.
The sunlight, still slippered,
Shone inside each leaf; alcoholic,
Illuminating and connecting
The glory to the glory.

The lawn was as sheer and blue
As ice. And hovering, with the uncertain grace of a gull
Three feet from the ground in the morning mist.
It cut one's throat, and only wanted
Someone's blood to be perfect.

And then the deer got up.

Aged 17
Playing the Violin

There is a crawling animal in the bottom somewhere.
It scudders at Mozart and snores at Bach.
Its eyes are as black and sticky as caviare,
And in between is its snout.

Mercy, little bear, little fable, or whatever
I am fated to call you;
Stay if you must, but come out if you can.
I shall then play such music
That you will be glad you went away.

It still remains; gently nuzzling the wood,
Occasionally chopping. And its eyes
Never grow dim as it follows the progress
Of my bow, and as it preens itself,
Mocking.

Brutus's Last Song

Caesar's back, and they built him a throne to sit on.
Get back to nature, Caesar. We've got you a tree stump
Broad as your kingly bottom. Magisterial,
Older than you'll ever be.
And when you rise from your wooden cradle
Black marks upon your robes'll tell the people where you've been.

Ah, but when you sit now, that's really something:
See that bush, like a marvellous African headdress
Full of yellow whips, their tops dipped with blood;
Or jugular red-hot pokers, who decided to take the day off
And wave a finger at your majesty.
Why, your majesty, see how, when you sit there,
They radiate around you.

One could almost believe you were going to die.

SIMON McMENZIE

Aged 14
He tried to kick the bucket, but had no legs

Simon McMenzie is 14, lives in Monkseaton, Whitley Bay, and goes to St Anselm's Roman Catholic High School in North Shields.

'My sense of humour is reflected in the poem, although I did not feel it would be popular with other readers, but there's no telling some people's taste.'

I'll tell you about a man
Who was once knocked down by an ice-cream van.
A crowd flocked there to see his pain,
The blood diluted by pouring rain.

An ambulance came to take him away
To the hospital, newly opened that day.
In this hospital, without a name
Lay the young man, unconscious and maimed.

When he came to, he tried to get out,
But had no legs, so began to shout,
'Doctor, nurse, come here to my bed,
And tell me what you have done to my legs.'

A nurse came in, full of charm;
The man tried to hit her, but he had no arms!
So there he lay, as good as dead,
A swaddled torso and a head.

His face went blue, his chest went red,
The nurse yelled out, 'I think he's dead!'
A doctor came in with all his "tools",
Examined, then said, 'This nurse is a fool.

While she was in here, as time passed by,
Her heavy foot covered his air supply.
Because of this, his lungs went dry,
But he couldn't tell the nurse quite why.
He spluttered, coughed, and quickly died.'

JONNY BUGG

Aged 9
Witch's Brew

Frogs or spiders, rats and snails,
People's heads and fingernails.
All the things get steaming hot,
With a little pinch of snot.

All the things make you feel sick,
A bit of seaweed does the trick,
Everything goes blacky green,
Really nasty to be seen.
The nasty smell's enough to throttle,
Until you put it in the bottle.

Jonny Bugg, now 12, goes to Gosforth Central Middle School. Reading Roald Dahl's books made him want to write himself. But he has to choose his subjects. One Hallowe'en at West Jesmond Juniors, this didn't happen: *'I dislike being given a bad title and told to write about it.'*

JONATHAN SCOULER

Aged 11
Witches

Three witches live in number 74,
The one with the big green door,
They eat boys and girls twice a day.
At Hallowe'en they go off on holiday.
Nobody knows where they go,
But scientific reasons show
They go hunting for the berries
      from the billyboatree
To make the poison E503.

Jonathan Scouler is 11, lives at Kingston Park and goes to Gosforth Central Middle School.
'I was inspired to write this after hearing a poem on witches read by my teacher Mrs Miller. I found the starting difficult but as I wrote it became easier. I enjoy humorous poems and limericks by Spike Milligan.'

JAMES LEGGOTT

Aged 10
Love at First Byte

I fell in love with my computer,
I knew it was love at first byte.
They said it was a syntax error
But I felt like a lovesick spryte.

Oh how I comm-adored it,
And on our first data-base
We were basically so dedicated,
And had beautiful interface.

They warned me about its peripherals,
And they thought I was taking a risk.
It was said to have bugs in its micros,
And would corrupt me with its floppy disk!

But we shared all our hardware and software,
I knew that our love would not break.
It was a case of chips with everything,
As we laughed till our Pixel would ache.

Then one day came a graphic lesson
I saw to my numeric shame,
There it was on display on a spreadsheet,
Linked to a mega mainframe!

It said they were just user friendly
And had never had any cad-cam.
But I had monitored its modem
And printed out each rom and ram.

I've managed to wipe off this memory,
I no longer cry 'Cursor for ever'.
I've met this cute compact disc player,
And we've started going round together.

James Leggott is 10, lives in Newcastle, and goes to the Royal Grammar. He plays piano and violin, and likes computers, chess and reading poetry, especially funny poems by Michael Rosen, Roger McGough and Spike Milligan.

'I'd written a few poems, but I decided to write a new one for the competition. I didn't have much success, so I thought it would be fun to write a poem about writing a poem.'

Aged 9
The Masterpiece

'Evening Chronicle Poetry Contest?'
This time I'm sure my entry will be best.
Off with the telly and other distractions,
No games, computer and video attractions.
Now here I sit listening to my Walkman blast,
(I wonder how long these batteries will last?)
Shall I write a poem that will rhyme?
I'd better think about it for some time.

Hmmm, there's not one idea that comes to mind.
No inspiration my brain can find.
I'm tired now I'll try another day.
No, no, don't give in, I can't delay.
The closing date is coming soon
So here I go – moon, June, balloon.

That's better. But the title maybe 'Christmas Time?'
Yes that's a good one, now for the first line.
'Christmas is coming, Christmas is coming,
Do diddle do, da humming? Strumming? Bumming?'
No that's no good, let's start again.
'Something, something, three wise men!'
Oh dear, this is getting worse,
Perhaps I'll never write a verse.

'I wandered lonely as a cloud'
No that will never be allowed.
What else? Nature? The City, maybe the sea?
Tall ships? Love? You and me?
Maybe the poem should not scan.
Then I can try to get as many words into a line as I possibly can.

I think I'll wait until next year for glory,
I've changed my mind, I'll write a story.

KIERAN OGDEN

Aged 11
Lucky Heather

She was always there every day,
Waiting for a passer-by who would buy her lucky heather.
'Lucky heather, buy my lucky heather,' she would say.
And she'd say the same every day, every weather,
'Buy my lucky heather.'

Sometimes I would buy some if I'd saved enough,
She would thank me with a voice so rough.
She would hand me the heather with a claw-like hand,
The rough twigs held closely by a rubber band.

Every day on the corner she'd sit in her rags,
With her big straw basket and her hessian bag.
When she's sold all her heather she'd wander away,
Singing 'I'd sell more heather but I've no more today.'

That one day last year she didn't appear,
She never came back but I feel she's near.
Because late at night I still can hear,
'Lucky heather, lucky heather' faintly in my ear.

Kieran Ogden lives in Tynemouth, and goes to St Anselm's Roman Catholic High School in North Shields. Now 12, she enjoys school 'for the social life of course'. This poem was written for English homework:

'As I was quite tired it only took me about 10 minutes to write. My favourite poems are ones by Spike Milligan and Roald Dahl. I enjoy writing poetry but only started because my friend liked it and at the time I did everything she did! How did I know it would end up like this!'